TRANSFORMATION
A Journey into Wholeness

Jeremi Harnack

All rights reserved. No portion of this publication may be reproduced, stored in a retrieval system, or transmitted in any form or by any means—electronic, mechanical, photocopy, recording, or otherwise—without prior written permission of the copyright owner.

Scripture Quotations
Unless otherwise noted, all Scripture quotations are from the Holy Bible, **New International Version**®, NIV® Copyright © 1973, 1978, 1984, 2011 by Biblica, Inc.® Used by permission. All rights reserved worldwide.

<u>Acronyms denote other versions used.</u>

The Holy Bible, **New King James Version** (NKJV) Copyright © 1982 Thomas Nelson. All rights reserved.

Holy Bible, **New Living Translation** (NLT) copyright © 1996, 2004, 2015 by Tyndale House Foundation. Used by permission of Tyndale House Publishers, Inc., Carol Stream, Illinois 60188. All rights reserved.

The Holy Bible, **Berean Study Bible** (BSB) Copyright ©2016, 2020 by Bible Hub Used by Permission. All Rights Reserved Worldwide.

Photos by permission of Pixabay.com, CC0 License, Public Domain, and Creative Commons, ShareAlike 3.0 Unported (CC BY-SA 3.0)

Printed in the United States of America
Copyright © Jeremi Harnack 2025
Published by JMH Publications 2025
Cover and Interior Design: C.A. Simonson
ISBN:ISBN: 979-8-218-67543-1

TABLE OF CONTENTS

ACKNOWLEDGEMENTS vii
PREFACE ix
LOVING 11
CHANGE ENCOUNTER 14
CHOSEN 15
PERSPECTIVES 19
LET GO 21
HOME AT LAST AFTER WANDERING FAR 23
PRINCE OF PEACE 28
CHAOS VERSUS LIGHT 29
ALTAR 31
SEEING MYSELF 33
A MAJOR DISCOVERY 35
ON THE AIR 37
WALKING 38
YOU LOVED ME 39
CHOICES 40
ASKING 44
THE GREAT COMMUNICATOR 46
YOU AND I 47
MEND ME 48
GROWN UP / FREEDOM 49
MY ON TIME GOD 52
POETRY ENCOUNTER 54

PRAYER OF A SURVIVOR	56
KEY TO TRANSFORMATION	57
PROVISION AND PROTECTION	59
DECISION	62
GOD OF LIFE	67
ALONE NOW	68
NEW CHILD	69
RESPONSE	70
OLD DEPTHS	71
NEW DEPTHS	71
INVERSION	72
POINT OF VIEW	73
PURPOSE FOR ME	74
WIND MEMORIES	76
GOD HUG	78
PROGRESS	80
TO BE	82
LANGUAGE ENCOUNTER	83
ADVENTURE	85
THE OTHER SIDE	86
DIVORCE	87
MY EVERYTHING GOD	89
WHERE AM I NOW?	90
BECOMING NOTHING	93
REASONS	95
BIRTHDAY GIFT	97

DREAMABLE	99
DREAMS	100
CHOOSING LIFE	101
YOU TOUCHED MY LIFE	104
AN OPPORTUNITY	105
ABOUT THE AUTHOR	107

ACKNOWLEDGEMENTS

I want to thank God and Jesus for bringing me through, not only the experiences, but also the writing and editing of this book.

And thanks are due to Renee Srch for encouraging and threatening me to get me to do this, and for guiding me through the process.

And thank you to my good friend, Julie Mendez, who puts up with my many quirks which result from not growing up at the right time.

And I want to acknowledge and thank Jill Harrison who played a crucial background role in this process.

PREFACE

Most of my writing has developed as a result of attempting to process who I was, how I got there and the changes that were happening, from initial salvation to a degree of Christian maturity. One approach would have been to present this in chronological order. That would have been simple enough as that was how much of it was originally written.

But this is not chapters in a book; it is a series of individual works many of which were developed or excerpted from the original writings in retrospect. I did a lot of necessary but painful filtering, to remove some of the heavier content which might not be appropriate for the general population, though some of it would hold value for a specialized audience. If you feel you need to see this material, I am willing to share it on an individual basis.

So, I decided not to go with the chronological arrangement, but to allow the material to stand as individual works. This may not be the most orderly presentation, but I believe it works for what I wanted, to highlight the depths of my difficulties while giving God the glory for walking with me through the problems and to bring me out into His glorious light.

LOVING

I was younger than the other girls,
As they talked in the dark of boys and LUV.
Not a subject I was "into" yet.
Alone and left out – again,
I listened quietly to the banter about she-loves-he.

Then came a thought, a voice,
"It's important to love and keep on loving...
Even when you get hurt,
Keep your heart open to love again."

Such a simple statement,
But not the wisdom of an early teen.
I didn't know then, Lord, that it was you,
Putting a guiding hand on my life.
Such a simple statement, but so <u>urgent,</u>
Impressing itself deeply in my heart

I tried, Lord,
It hung in my mind that keeping an open heart
Was a most important task.
But hurts came and walls were built
Even when I tried not to hide.
Then, refusing to shrivel up inside,
 I slowly took the walls apart and
 Learned to love again, and again.

Then, just when it got too hard,
When I felt, love or no love,
The struggle was hardly worth it,
When having enough of everything except love
Felt like having nothing at all,
You introduced Yourself to me and offered me love.
I took it and ran.

And you began to show me what real love is.
You held and comforted me
Over those past broken hearts.
You showed me the scars and the walls
That I didn't know were still there,
And You took them all away.

You gave me purpose and direction in my life
You made me whole.
Today, the joy, peace, fulfillment,
Contentment and excitement
Your love has brought to me,
Are the stuff of legends.
Never a man loved a woman as completely
And wonderfully as You do, Lord.

I think back, sometimes, about that night.
What if it had never happened!
And I cry, to think how I would have died inside
A long time ago.
There wouldn't have been any _me_ left
To accept that wonderful offer of love
If it hadn't been for those simple words,
Whispered by You that dark night, long ago.

The beauty and depth of your caring,
And the length of Your loving arm,
Amaze me so,
That your praise wells up inside me
And bursts forth in song,
A song of love to my God
Who knows the end from the beginning
Whose love encompasses me
Through all the years.

I love You, Lord.

CHANGE ENCOUNTER

I remember my first poem in high school.
It was called "Loneliness", and it was good.
So good the nuns gave me a prize, a missal.
So real they changed my room—
From a private room to a dorm.
But they never talked to me about it.

Today, I remember the truth of that poem,
That you can be lonely in a crowd,
When the loneliness lives inside you.
But I don't remember, now,
Those feelings in my heart.

Oh, yes, my mind knows how lonely I was,
A little kid in a boarding school,
Away from family, without any friends.
But my heart, today, is so full of You, Lord,
I'm unable to feel that loneliness as real.

You have filled up every nook and cranny of my life
With the reality of You and Your love.
I know that, now, no matter what happens,
I'll never be that kind of lonely again.
I have you, now. What a change, Lord!

What a glorious, happy change!

CHOSEN

There was a day when I could not function because I had not resolved my pain over the circumstances of my life. There was a day when I felt that the death of my mother was the ruination of my life. It was a day when I thought my years spent in boarding school away from any normal familial relationships was unpardonable cruelty. There was a day when I felt that a life full of rejection and isolation was not worth living. That day is no more! God has healed the pain of those woundings, and I realize I might never have been able to come to salvation if I had been in other circumstances.

Today is another day.

Today I realize God is using all my past woundings to bring me to a place I could not otherwise have come. Today I realize He has chosen me for a purpose. He named me Jeremi, which means "chosen of God". And I finally realized that He planned that name long before I was born. It was 80 years between the time that my father picked up the nickname of Jerry until I became an adult and accepted that the name the catholic nuns had made from the mess my father had put on my birth certificate, Jeremi, was actually what God meant for me to be named in the first place.

For many years I sought out what God's purpose in choosing me was, without much revelation. I had talents and gifts, and I used them, but no sense of purpose with a passion attached. Then one evening as I listened to a Christian song that I had heard and sung for years, I realized that the name it used for Jesus was "The Chosen One". He was chosen to be our deliverer, but He was wounded. From a birth in poverty and disgrace, through a life of rejection and ridicule, to a horrific death meant for the worst criminals, He was wounded throughout His life. Even though He had a visible ministry, He was called Beelzebub (the devil) by the Jewish leadership, and betrayed by one of His chosen ones, and killed by His own people.

I realized that being chosen of God is not about some specific ministry. It is about relationship and service. If God could wound His own Son, Jesus, the Chosen One, so severely, why should I expect anything less of Him in my life. In fact, being wounded is a part of being chosen. Jesus was already perfect, conceived of the Holy Spirit. I am far from perfect. Even after the refinings I have been through, I need much work to be molded into the one God wants me to be.

> *"Come near to God and He will come near to you."*
>
> James 4:8a

I could, before that particular night, intellectually say, "What are the woundings of Jeremi, 'chosen of God', compared to those of Jesus?" But it was that night I began to know in my heart that my woundings were a part of God's choosing of me. They were not just cruel accidents or things put upon me by others. They were a part of a special path that God allowed me to walk, to bring me to the place He desired, one which would make me wholly committed to Him. Each wounding had a purpose, some to bring me to the Lord, some to help me to grow up, some to help me become aware of new aspects of my relationship with God.

Many people do not like to hear that God would wound anyone. How do they deal with the fact that an  all-knowing, loving, and totally in control God sent His special Son to earth specifically to die so that others might live? I don't have a problem with this because I have come to the place to give "permission" for my past treatment, for I know the character of the God I serve. I know His loving nature, His all-knowing mind, and His ability to take anything that happens and turn it into a rich gem that gives glory to Him, and turns us into shining stars, testifying to His goodness. And God surely knew the one He was choosing and forming would be willing to "give permission" once she was made aware of what He was doing.

For now, until God gives more revelation, my special ministry for God is to be me. It is to live my life as fully as possible, looking always to Him, and to worship and praise Him for all that comes into my life, whether I see it as good or as bad. My name is Jeremi, chosen of God, and I wouldn't have it any other way.

PERSPECTIVES

The change was momentous,
An earthquake, or so it seemed to me.
I could feel such a difference,
As though my whole world were new.
Everything was beautiful, and I was free.

I was amazed to realize that others
Didn't see the change at all,
Only the same old me.
How could it be?
Why didn't they know what I knew?
Didn't it show?

As far as ever we travel, there's always farther to go. As much as ever we learn, there's always more to know.
What looks so huge to us from up close,
Is next to invisible,
From the great distance of another person's eyes.

It isn't that they're blind or don't care.
It's just that even those closest to us
Come to everything with a
Different point of view from ours.
It's like looking at opposite sides of the same mountain.
It's about as annoying as anything can be.

> *"Being confident of this, that He who began a good work in you will carry it on to completion until the day of Christ Jesus."*
>
> **Philippians 1:6**

And your hurt is real and deep,
When they can't see what you know is there.
But God wants to be sure we know our journey
Isn't over yet.

Each "earthquake" is but a single step
On the long road of transformation,
And the biased eyes of those around us,
Only serve to show us just how far we have to go.

As far as ever we travel, there's always farther to go.
As much as ever we learn, there's always more to know.
What looks so huge to us from up close,
Is next to invisible,
From the great distance of another person's eyes.

LET GO

What, Lord? You say it's time for You
To be in charge of me?
To let that little girl inside put down
Her heavy load,
So both of us can finally grow?
But it's so hard, Lord,
To let go of all those child-made methods,
That helped me when I hurt so badly.
They're my survival.

If I let go of them, it feels
As though I'll die for sure.
They *must* be right, they're how I made it
All the way to here.
To give them up would mean to. . .No!
I can't, Lord, I'd go crazy,
I'd split into a million
pieces. It's *too* hard.

What, Lord?
You mean those very techniques
I used for survival,
Are the things that are
Causing all the pain?
Are you sure, Lord?
Hold me close, Lord.

You're the only light I see.

"Trust in the Lord with all your heart and lean not on your own understanding; in all your ways submit to Him and He will make your paths straight."

Proverbs 3:5-6

HOME AT LAST AFTER WANDERING FAR

Home at last, after wandering far. What joy, what peace! It is a release from heavy burdens and a salvation from desperate circumstances. I have been blessed to experience such a homecoming more than once in my life. They were similar experiences, yet there was a most important difference between them.

My first such homecoming occurred in August, 1975, when I flew into the Baltimore Airport and I spotted my husband, Bob, in the welcoming crowd. He was my husband of six weeks and we had spent all but the first two days of our marriage separated by almost two thousand miles. He had been home in Maryland, writing his doctoral dissertation, and I had been in Texas, in the Air Force, struggling desperately to get back home.

When I signed my letter of intent to enter the Air Force, Bob and I had known each other only a few weeks. By the time I had to leave to go wandering far away in Texas for training, we knew we wanted to marry. We planned to get married the following year, when he would have his PhD and be settled into his first professional position. We had no idea that the institutional nature of the Air Force would thrust me into emotional turmoil, triggering painful memories of a childhood spent in boarding school, making me fear for my emotional survival. When we realized the severity of my response, we knew I had to get out of the Air Force.

Bob flew down to Texas; we had a quick courthouse wedding and the briefest of honeymoons, before he returned to his battle with his dissertation back in Maryland. I, equipped with our certificate of marriage, and both armed with and hindered by my emotional state, began to battle the Air Force for an honorable humanitarian discharge. After six weeks of battle, I was spending hours each day in tears and was failing my training classes. Then, suddenly, the Air Force released me. They could not station me within their own distance limits of where my husband had taken a permanent position. I was summarily put on a plane home, honorable discharge in hand.

Coming through the passenger entrance and searching the crowds for Bob's face. I still felt apprehensive. Maybe I'm just dreaming that I'm coming home, maybe my release from the Air Force was just a joke, maybe my husband of six weeks (or two days) won't be here. But there he was! I was really home! The battle was over. I could relax and we could start our life together. As I ran weeping into his open arms, the intensity of joy made me alternately want to shout out loud to tell all the world, and to find a most private place to handle the too private feelings. Emotion piled on top of emotion, and I wept my way through the layers.

As glorious as this homecoming was, it was a passing event. After a while, the flush of emotion faded, and life continued as usual. Over the next months, we clung to one another constantly, dreading separation. We had to consciously work to overcome the fear. We still had battles to win, Bob's PhD and his new job, and our new relationship to establish. Over time, new problems arose, problems my human savior could not solve. And our marriage progressed only a little better than one would expect considering its bent and rocky start.

Eight years later, my next such homecoming occurred in a Holiday Inn meeting room that was being used for Sunday services by a local church. That lovely day I glimpsed Jesus, arms open, waiting for me to run to Him. Until then, I had only been told of Jesus, but I believed in Him. Only once, many years before, in a "chance" and passing conversation had anyone mentioned having a relationship with Jesus. But that once had been enough to put the desire for such a thing into my heart. I had not known that it also had been enough for Jesus to permanently claim me as His own.

With no real knowledge or support to nurture my desire for a relationship with Jesus, I wandered far during the next twenty years. The world constantly tried to train me to think its way. As an adult, emotional problems that psychologists could not seem to solve, plagued me. I struggled to win the war of just surviving life, but, without Jesus, I kept losing the battles. Yes, I got married. I had a job, a home and a family, all the things the world labels as success. But my husband/savior could not solve the deep emotional problems within me that kept me in depression and anxiety, despite my apparent success. After years of seeking a solution, I was almost ready to take medications which might have given me peace for a while. However, they would have destroyed my body in about ten years. I was desperate for peace, at the end of my rope. Yet I couldn't even understand that peace was what I needed.

And then, I walked into that meeting room, and I glimpsed Jesus. I could feel His presence in the service, and He spoke into my heart that I could run to Him for refuge. So, I did! The pastor prayed with me, and I asked Jesus to come into my heart. Jesus' embrace was as real to me as my husband's had been eight years before. Jesus released me from my desperate struggle and took my emotional burdens from me. Joy and peace flowed over me as I accepted the love of my new Savior and set out to establish a new life with Him. And, yes, I cried my way through those piles of emotions, also.

This reunion, however, had a most important difference from the first one. After the first emotional flush faded this time, I was left, not with a fallible human savior, but with Jesus, omnipotent Savior, Emmanuel, God with us. He could solve all problems, even ones I didn't know I had. When problems came that I needed to go through, He was always there, to hold my hand or carry me on His strong shoulders. After the first emotional flush faded, I found myself wrapped in the arms of Jesus, the Son of the God, who is Love, capable of loving me at my worst, and then forgiving and healing the sin and hurts that put me there. After the first emotional flush faded, I found I had put myself under the authority of one who desired to empower me with His authority. After the first emotional flush faded, I found I had been eternally bound to one who desired a deep and abiding, intimate relationship with me.

In truth, the emotional flush has never really faded at all. This second home coming has lasted 41 years, so far, and there is no shadow of turning to be seen. Each day, as I interact with the world, and get busy with worldly tasks, there is the tiniest sense of "traveling far," but, the moment I sit quietly again in the presence of God in prayer, I am once again, "home at last", filled with the joy and peace of Jesus's salvation and love.

PRINCE OF PEACE

The handsome window salesman
On my living room chair
Had turned out to be a pastor.
He spoke of God in a way
I had not heard of before,
And I heard him say
"He wants to give you peace."

It hit home!
Peace was what I needed.
It was the missing piece.
I couldn't believe I'd gone so long
Never realizing what it was I needed.

If knowing Jesus could bring me peace,
What more could I ever ask?
The hunger, the need, was so great!

I took the bait. I was hooked.
You reeled me into shore.
And when I landed in Your
hands,
You gave me that peace
And so much more.
How can I thank the Fisher of Men
For being the Prince of Peace.

"And He will be called Wonderful Counselor, Mighty God, Everlasting Father, Prince of Peace."

Isaiah 9:6b

CHAOS VERSUS LIGHT

Chaos is craziness, torment and fear
Not knowing what's wrong or why it's wrong.
It's a deep pit full of unpleasant things
Hidden deep in the innermost mind.

It's fear and crying and a scream inside that goes on and on,
Never stopping but covered up and hidden away.
It's being a child that never grows up,
Locked forever in that place of horror and hurt and helplessness.

It's a mind that's crowded with people yet always alone,
Craving a love it has never known.
It's hanging on longer,
Waiting and hoping that something will change.

It's disorder and pain and darkness
It's death without dying and living without life.

* * * * * *

Light is what comes in and sends the darkness away.
It's peace, and love, and life, and growth, and joy. It's restoration and renewal.

It's active, ongoing, continuing, exciting,
Fulfilling and satisfying.
It's thirsting and having your thirsting quenched
All in the same moment.

It's dancing when the only music is the fragrance
Of incense that is praise to the Lord.
It's a flat plain where you can run forever
And know you are safe.

It's freedom to live and be real to yourself
And that self is something good to be.
It's knowing you are finally growing,
And going somewhere that's a good place to go.

It's being free to let go of the pain
And accept the joy that only God can give.
It's knowing there's One
Who cares for you with a love that is real
Not bent to his own selfish concerns.

It's knowing a Holy God knows you so well,
All the darkness and dirt you've walked through,
Yet He's willing to call you His own.
It's the love of Jesus deep in your heart,
Cleansing and healing all the hurts of the past.

> *"Jesus answered, 'I am the way the truth and the life. No one comes to the Father except through me.'"*
>
> John 14:6

ALTAR

It seems like defeat in a way,
I had so set my heart on a wonderful goal,
And it seems I should have had it in hand.
To turn away and search somewhere else
Is giving up, isn't it?
This is where the goal should be.
Why isn't it here? Why can't I see?

God, please help me.
You know how much, and what, I need.
Your word has promised me it would be mine.
Show me how I can give up hope, and still
Receive the promise.

> *"Take your son, your only son, whom you love, Isaac, and go to the region of Moriah. Sacrifice him there as a burnt offering on a mountain I will show you."*
>
> Genesis 22:2

Abraham and Isaac!
Take that thing that's dearest to me,
The very means by which I should,
See fulfillment of the promise you gave,
And put it on the altar to give it back to you,
With all intent focused on allowing you
To take back the very thing you gave,
Knowing from the depths of my spirit
That, having given the promise,

You will not revoke it,
Even though all the apparent means for
Fulfilling it are taken away.
Somehow, there will be a lamb caught in a bush,
Or the promise will come true in a way
I couldn't possibly foresee.

Lord, if I know this is what You ask of me
I can do it. But in no other way can I
Let go of this dream.
Tell me it's You who takes it away,
And I can bear any loss.

You do ask it? I will do it!
Oh Lord, was it only a moment ago
That my dream seemed so important?
But now, You fill my field of vision,
And I am content.

> *"...now I know that you fear God, because you have not withheld your son from me..."*
>
> *"Abraham looked up and there in a thicket he saw a ram caught by its horns. He went over and took the ram and sacrificed it as a burnt offering instead of his son."*
>
> Genesis 22:12b-13

SEEING MYSELF

> *"Call to me and I will answer you and tell you great and unsearchable things you do not know."*
>
> Jeremiah 33:3

First, I saw the need,
That something *had* to change!
"No longer can I go on like this.
But he won't change. Help, Lord!"

Then I saw You, my Lord.
You want to help me, Lord?
You want to change me, Lord?
But why change me?
Isn't he the one who needs it?
You'll see, child.
And see I did, finally.

I saw all the hurts and sins and knots,
Buried deep within my broken heart.
I saw I hated his problems so,
Because they threatened
My own self-imposed blindness.

I saw all the ways
The faults I saw in him,
Were little more than different faces
On my own failings.
I saw my own massive
Mountains of difficulties

Made his problems look like
Tiny specks of sand.

I saw I was bound up, and tied up,
And locked into places
I didn't want to be.
I saw the truth.

Then I saw You
Set Me Free!
Hallelujah!!
Thank You, Lord!

"Guide me in your truth and teach me, for you are God my Savior and my hope is in you all day long."

Psalm 25:5

A MAJOR DISCOVERY

It would be a trial-and-error process, but when they found the right combination of drugs, it would help me be more functional, peaceful, for a while. However, the drugs would destroy my body in about 10 years. The psychologist made an appointment for me to begin the testing.

Fortunately, God prevented that by showing me His Son, Jesus. I was 34 when I became a Christian. I began to experience the healing love of God in my life, began to grow in Christ and was cured of the depression and anxiety.

But God warned me that I would experience some of these things again. I understood that I needed to have confidence that the underlying problems were taken care of. So that first healing miracle did not resolve all my problems. Though I had Jesus in my heart, so that it was easier to deal with difficulties, He would have to do yet more miracles to bring me to full function.

I was 44 years old before I finally discovered through Christian counseling and psychological care that I had responded to my childhood trauma, one lonely 6-year-old day, by exploding myself into a million pieces, and creating personalities inside myself for every scary little event in my life, keeping each problem small and separate to protect against further explosions. Energy that should have gone into living went into managing these people within me. And there weren't just people, but also, a deep pit full of unspeakable things in my mind. I was basically crazy and had spent 40 years trying not to live my life.

> *"For those God foreknew He also predestined to be conformed to the image of His Son, that He might be the firstborn among many brothers and sisters."*
>
> Romans 8:29

From that day, it took 18 months of intense psychological and spiritual care, bringing each person and creature in my mind to deliverance through prayer, before I could say that God, by His Divine Mercy, had healed most of that craziness. It took letting go of many things I did not want to release. It took taking responsibility for my own decisions and learning to forgive others for the ways they failed me. It took learning new ways to think and act and respond to problems, while holding on to Jesus for dear life.

I still sometimes struggle with overcoming old habits and thought patterns, but I can now say my head acknowledges the craziness that used to live within, but my heart rejoices because the darknesses are gone. The joy of the new life I live in Jesus is worth the journey I have taken to be able to find that life.

ON THE AIR

How many times, as I travel through this life,
Trying to smell the roses,
I catch a whiff of things not so sweet.

Of course, I complain of how
The world is going to pot.
I close my nose, shut myself off,
Try to get away from it,
Avoiding the truth that part of the stench
Is coming from me.

My problem is I keep walking around
With the same old bag of garbage,
Thinking I can avoid the smell.
But waste is waste.
Sooner or later
I'm going to be exposed.

> *"But if we walk in the light as He is in the light, we have fellowship with one another, and the blood of Jesus, His Son, purifies us from all sin."*
>
> 1 John 1:7

The answer's simple.
Dump the stuff that causes the smell.
Give it to Jesus, let Him clean me up,
As His Word assures me He can.

Then I can breathe a fresher air
Than ever I imagined,
And the odor I'll have will be
The sweetness of Jesus' salvation
And His cleansing power.

WALKING

Slowly, Lord, you led me out of my hurt,
To a place where I could stand.
Leaning heavily on your arm,
I began to try to take some steps.
Just acknowledging the need for change
Seemed to work a change in me.

And you were gentle.
You knew me well.
You told me what I needed to know.
But you didn't tell me, then, what would
Have crushed my spirit, if heard too soon.
All the things I was afraid of
Had already happened, and I saw it not.
I WAS already crazy,
And split into a million pieces.
Instead, you took it slowly, gently,
Unwrapping one gloriously weepy
Onion layer at a time,
Until you had me walking with You,
One person, one place,
On the road to surviving survival.

YOU LOVED ME

You loved me ere I ever knew You.
You formed me in the womb,
And brought me forth,
According to Your plan.
You knew me from the inside out,
Long before I was born.
You put your hand on me,
Saving my life
From first breath on.

I can't count the times
You've saved me,
Even before I had the sense
To know it was You,
Before I knew how much
I needed to be grateful to You.

So, now as I look back
Over Your wonders in my life,
I want to express my thanks,
To You, the God of the Universe.
For Your love, mercy, grace,
Kindness and patience.

Thank You for Your goodness,
For being, truly, the all-powerful God,
For whom all things are possible.
Thank You for so much more
Than I can ever say.

> *"We love because He first loved us."*
> 1 John 4:19

CHOICES

I had choices.

We all tend to feel we got into these fixes
Because of what others did to us,
And while others certainly did things
They shouldn't have done,

I did have choices.

When faced with a world
I didn't know how to handle,
I could have just let it all overwhelm me,
And gone <u>completely</u> crazy,
Ended up in an institution
Or, maybe gotten healed.

But I didn't.

I could have become bitter,
Let my anger and hurt rule my life,
Struck out against others,
And spread the pain to their lives, too.

But I didn't.

Or I could have cried out to others for help.
If I had let that scream inside of me
Come out for someone else to hear,
Maybe they would have understood,

Seen the world from where I was standing,
And given me the hugs and caring
I so desperately needed.
They might have even tried to help me understand.

But I didn't.

I could even have cried out to God.
I know, now, that it was a possibility,
But at six years old, I didn't know
He was a God who could or would
Be willing to help.

So, I didn't.

Instead, I chose to hold some part of me together,
To struggle on with living in a world I didn't understand.
I chose not to strike out at others,
Even in the midst of the chaos that I felt.
I chose to hide the craziness inside,
Away even from myself.

I did not know the path I chose
Would take me where I went,
It wasn't a place I would choose to go.
But the pain that I experienced,
And the wanderings I made,
Have brought me finally to that blessed place

Of knowing the love of God.

It wasn't fair that the things
That happened to me did.
The ones who caused me pain should have known
Better than to do the things they did.
But I have not lived the life I lived
Because of what others did to me.

I had choices.

I had choices.
At each step along the way I made a choice.
And, good or bad, dumb or smart, right or wrong,
The choices were my own.
They are what determined
The way I responded to the world.

None of us has full control
Over how we live our lives
Other things and people will impact themselves on us.
And there are limits to our choices.

But we can make a choice about
Who we want to be inside.
How we treat our friends and enemies and God,
If we want to love or hate,
Or isolate ourselves from it all.

    I had choices, you have them too.

You can choose to try to do it all yourself
Or let God take care of you.
I recommend the latter.

I chose to struggle on my own so many years,
And shed so many tears
I know, now, I needn't have cried,
'Til I gave the battle up to God,
And found the peace I needed in His loving care.

ASKING

I heard from the man that God could give me peace.
If I had peace, what more could I ask?
So, I asked You into my life
And You gave me that peace.
What more could I ask, indeed!
When You gave me peace you let me see
How great was the need for everything else.

You showed me the hurt that others had done.
You showed me the pain I had hidden away.
You showed me my need for love and growth.
You showed me how You could heal it all.

Along with peace you gave me hope,
And joy and life and light.

You opened my heart
and eyes and ears.
To hear your wondrous,
loving voice
To respond to the
beauty of who You are,
The God of the
universe.

> *"Jesus looked at them and said, 'with man this is impossible, but with God all things are possible'".*
>
> Matthew 19:26

I'd said I wouldn't ask for more,
But now I see I was wrong in that.
You want us to ask, seek, desire
All the wonders you have for us.

When we ask for more of Your sweet self,
We fill your fondest desire.

And so I asked, and You've encouraged,
Baiting me to ask You for more.
And as I've asked You've given and given,
Till now You've healed my heart,
And given me peace to a deeper degree
Than I knew how to ask.

Yay God!

THE GREAT COMMUNICATOR

The great communicator!

Right!

What kind of communication is
it when frustration raises the
voice
and anger fills the tone?

As though his ears were the problem,
and one could shout anything into the
heart?
Maybe we've overestimated our skills
in the communication department
just a wee bit,
hmm?

**Help me, Lord!
Pleeease!**

YOU AND I

You and I, Lord,
That's what it all comes down to,
You and I.
I come to You, and I say "They", Lord.
You hold and comfort and console.
Then, softly, gently, You say, "**you**."

I, Lord? But They!
"*I know about them,*" You say,
　　　"*but you.*"
But they'll get away with . . .
"*I can take care of them,* **you**."

But. . . *"you."*
Bu-ut. . . *"you."*
Bu-bu-but. . . *"you."*
OK. Lord, whatever You say.
What do you mean by me, Lord?
And then, You showed me,
And helped me to change.

Then, I saw that things were different.
I know I changed, but did they change, too?
Or am I just looking at everything,
From a new point of view.

> *"Why do you look at the speck of sawdust in your brother's eye and pay no attention to the plank in your own eye?"*
>
> Matthew 7:3

> *"If we confess our sins, He is faithful and just to forgive us our sins and to cleanse us from all unrighteousness."*
>
> 1 John 1:9

MEND ME

My dearest Savior, forgive me for my hiding.
I repent and want to change my ways.
I never want to hide again.

Dear Jesus,
Please mend me, sew up my holes.
Make me a garment that you can wear.
No tears and no pockets, no hidden places,
But clean and fresh and all of one piece.
And let me walk in your light and your truth,
As I learn more to love all of your ways,
Staying close by your side all of my days.

Thank you, Lord.

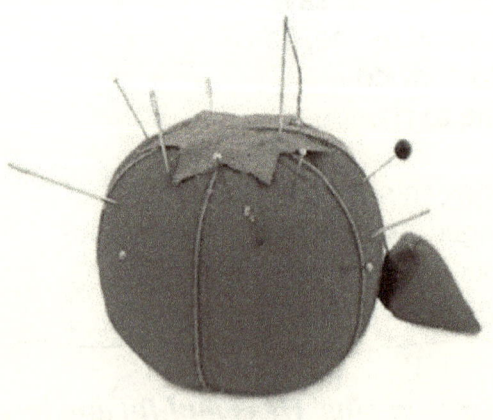

GROWN UP / FREEDOM

> *"It is for freedom that Christ has set us free. Stand firm, then, and do not let your lives be burdened again by a yoke of slavery."*
>
> Galatians 5:1

Grown up feels good.
It feels like freedom.
Not freedom *from* the rules,
But freedom to use the rules to make choices
I've never been able to make before.

It's freedom to *want* to do
What I'm supposed to do,
To accept the challenge, actively,
To do a job that I don't like,
Well enough that I learn to like it enough to do it well.
It's freedom to find pleasure in the pleasure of others,
Rather than just in what I want for myself.

It's freedom to see the other side,
To let go of the tensions that made me
Need to be the only one who was right.
Even the freedom to admit I'm wrong, now and then,
So I can learn to be right.

Grown up is freedom from being locked into childhood,
From wanting to grow
But not knowing how to do it on my own.
It's freedom to know I can still be a child sometimes,

Because my God is big enough to run things
And hold me at the same time.
And it's freedom to choose to be adult again,
Even though it's hard,
Because it stretches me and makes me grow some more.

> *"You, my brothers and sisters, were called to be free. But do not use your freedom to indulge the flesh; rather serve one another humbly in love."*
>
> Galatians 5:13

It's freedom to start to see who I am,
And freedom to continue to grow and change
Into a new and better me,
Because I can see that that's what I need.

Grown up is freedom mixed with responsibility.
It's a taking on of burdens I know I have to carry,
And knowing they're worth the effort
Knowing that life will be sweeter in the long run
for what I give to others now.

It's knowing which responsibilities are mine,
And which are not.
And it's the acceptance of the responsibility
That truly gives the freedom.
It's freedom to know that life's not all sweet,

But that even the bitter tastes better later,
Sometimes better than all the sweet in the world.
Grown up is freedom to love a complex God
And to seek to know Him in depth.
It's freedom to trust Him even when the path he shows

Looks hard and rough.

It's freedom to praise Him
For the pain as well as for the pleasure,
For the deepest cuts have resulted
In the loveliest lines
As He has sculpted me with His loving hand.

> *"Now, the Lord is the Spirit, and where the Spirit of the Lord is, there is freedom."*
>
> 2 Corinthians 3:17

MY ON TIME GOD

The incessant crying of my seven-day-old daughter had brought me just about to my wits' end. As a first-time mother at 35, I was inexperienced with children of any age, tended to overreact to loud or sustained noises, particularly under stress, and had given birth by C-section. My daughter had been crying for hours, I was in pain, and I could feel my control slipping away. However, I had no way to get away, and there was no one else, at that moment, to care for her. I was seconds away from hurting my child. I needed a way out – fast!

I threw my hands in the air, lifted my eyes, and cried out, "Lord, this is Your child. Help! If you don't intervene right now, I'm liable to hurt her." The next moment the phone rang. I stormed to the phone, answered in a barely civil tone, and heard my husband say he was coming home early. Was there anything I needed? "Yes! Get here as fast as possible." He prayed with me, and when I hung up, I was calm. God had instantly answered my prayer. In fact, He had prepared the answer before I even prayed.

But He had given more than a momentary victory. As I held my daughter close, I realized I never again had to feel that same desperation. I knew that I was never truly alone, that all God's resources were available to me in a whisper. The victory I experienced that day was permanent. My daughter is now a grown woman, who was never abused by an exasperated mother.

> *"Before they call, I will answer; while they are yet speaking, I will hear."*
>
> Isaiah 65:24

POETRY ENCOUNTER

You're cute, Lord, Is that irreverent, Sir?
But really, you are!
You knew the whole thing from the beginning,
You planned it.
And you carried it off with the greatest of style.

There I was, not even suspecting.
I just went along, blind to it all,
Thinking it random, not gathering it in.
You arranged it all, bit by bit,
Then brought all the pieces together for me.
Now that I see it, my surprise is the greater,
For not having guessed as I went along.

From the beginning you filled me up with music.
But you gave me no way to let it out
Singing, dancing, piano went nowhere.
Writing? Disorganized!
And I had nothing to write about.
No, that's not entirely true.
But how could I write what I couldn't admit?

Then I heard your voice, felt your touch,
Saw your healing in my life.
Slowly, things began to change.
You gave me hints, now, as we went along.
Of something special, but not what it was
And, still, I had music locked inside.

You asked for more, you asked for surrender
And when I obeyed,
I fell head-over-heels,
Wonderfully, hopelessly, permanently
In love with you.
And you let the music loose.

Now I have poetry pouring out of me,
Like a waterfall.
Everything's a poem, and every poem
Is a splash of water,
Rushing to leap off the cliff edge,
Into the mighty, powerful pool of your praise.

You gave me a gift, Lord, a wonderous gift.
But you held it back 'til just the right time,
The time you wanted,
The best time for us both.
The moment when the only way I'd want to use it.
Would be to bring you glory, Lord.
Wonderful, Lord.

See what I mean by saying you're cute, Lord?
Sitting there waiting forty-eight years
To spring this on me!
You were probably chortling most of the time.
I just hope my joy and delight,
Now that I see your hand,
Have made the wait worthwhile for you.
They have for me!

Thank you, Lord

PRAYER OF A SURVIVOR

Lord, you know who and how I am.
If I could do this myself, I would give it a try.
But I know that I need your wisdom and power
To open my eyes to all the ways
I fall into the old traps.
It's scary and hard to live life for real,
Instead of playing hit-and-run
With life and responsibility.

Give me your courage,
To keep in touch with life.
Give me your strength to stay,
Where I've always run away.
Give me your endurance,
Where habit has begotten laziness.
Give me your love of life,
Where I have succumbed to fear.

> *"The Lord our God is merciful and forgiving, even though we have rebelled against Him."*
>
> Daniel 9:9

> *"Great is our Lord and mighty in power; His understanding has no limit."*
>
> Psalm 147:5

And most of all my dearest Lord,
Give me your forgiveness,
For the fool I've been,
And your healing for the pain
I've caused myself,
By not wanting to change,
And not seeing through those rotten lies.
Thank you, Lord, for opening my eyes.

KEY TO TRANSFORMATION

In putting together this book on transformation, I have tried to not drag readers through all the angst I experienced in this process, but in minimizing the angst, it sometimes seems a bit too glib and easy. As if just saying Jesus is Lord solves everything. In one sense that is true, and in many cases we see miraculous changes and healing take place instantly, as it did with me receiving a new experience of peace at the time of my salvation. But we are fallen people and often we put up resistance to the very things that we need to get where we say we want to go. I did not even understand at that time that there was somewhere more I needed to go. And the enemy wants to block us at every turn.

To overcome this situation, we need to be able to accept some deep and difficult changes. And God wants us to have a heart attitude which actively cooperates with Him as He works in us. For me, the key to everything has been my prayer life. I am so far from perfect, but God allowed me to come to a place of intimacy in prayer which is best expressed in the following poem on prayer.

PRAYER

Contact, communion, comfort, life.
Food and drink, intimacy beyond compare.
Excitement, quiet peace, warfare, victory.
Joy beyond bearing, grief to overwhelm the soul.
Purpose, power, forgiveness, love.

Essence of life, a way to live,
Wrapped in and surrounded by the presence of God.
At home at last after wandering far,
Hidden, protected and safe.

A secret between my God and me
That's so special and private,
It lights up my life each day.
Yet the secret can be known by any who care
To reach out for Your outstretched hand.

Relationship, trust, responsibility, growth.
Delight in one another.
A love story passing back and forth
Between the Maker and the work of His hand.

    Transformation is not the result of some formula or series of works. Transformation comes from close, intimate, moment-by-moment relationship with the God of the universe and His Son, Jesus Christ, where we recognize that God knows better than we and we allow Him to tell us what we need.

PROVISION AND PROTECTION

"I will provide everything you need."
That's all He said. But it's not all I heard.

I heard that I needed to remember that, though my husband, Bob, has been God's means of providing for and protecting me for 30 years, God, Himself, is the provider and protector.

I heard that even if my situation or circumstances should change, God still will be my provider and protector.

I heard that His statement was all-encompassing. Nothing that I could ever need was left out of the promise.

I heard that my circumstances would change in some significant way, but that I could face those changes in the fullness of joy, for it would all be according to His infinitely perfect plan for me and others.

> *"And my God will meet all your needs according to the riches of His glory in Christ Jesus."*
>
> Philippians 4:19

I heard that God, the Creator of the Universe, cared deeply for me, deeply enough to answer the question before I knew to ask it, and deeply enough to calm my fears before they could arise. Is this not the essence of the longing of the human heart, to have someone care for us, to want to provide for us and protect us? Oh, the deep peace and contentment that enters the soul when the matter of being cared for is settled. Oh, the absolute joy of knowing the One who cares is so completely able to both provide and protect. There is a strange and beautiful contentment that comes from knowing that no matter what great, normally overwhelming, event should overtake us, we will not only survive, but thrive, because we are being held in the palm of God's hand. Lord, how can I thank you for the joy of your love!

I heard this personal promise from God 26 years ago, and since then my circumstances have significantly changed more than once. I saw my marriage both renew itself and then crumble. Over time, I lost everything and had to fight my way back to stability. But the Lord was there with me every step of the way. I saw God open doors for me to recover, in ways beyond my ability to imagine. And in times when I forgot this precious promise and wanted to give it all up, He was right there to tell me that He loved me, and because I loved Him, He wanted me to live. He has, indeed, provided everything I have needed over this entire time, and He, still today, continues to provide for me in every circumstance.

Even today, as we face attempts to destroy our country, to put us under even more oppressive rule, to destroy our financial system, to ruin the lives of our children, to push more and more against the God of the Bible, the Lord is protecting those who love Him, even as He judges the evil that is coming against His people.

He comes to us with a constant theme of "Do not fear!" There is no end to His resources, or His desire to provide for and protect each and every one of us. Will you allow Him to do that for you?

> *"The Lord is my rock, my fortress and my deliverer; my God is my rock, in whom I take refuge."*
>
> *2 Samuel 22:2-3*

DECISION

"How will we ever get this mess resolved? What can we do to turn this disaster of a marriage into a Christian relationship?" I had been asking myself this regularly for months. My husband and I were barely talking, and what we were saying wasn't friendly by any stretch of the imagination. Divorce was out of the question because of our belief in Jesus, and there was no hitting allowed. But those were the only real limits on our expressions of dissatisfaction with our relationship.

We had been going to counseling for a while, then my husband had stopped going and I was totally exasperated. It looked like the bottom of the barrel to me, but I didn't know that the Lord had one more surprise in store for me.

One Sunday our pastor, who knew the situation well, came over to offer some comfort for my obvious distress. Earlier, I requested that he try to hear from the Lord for me, because I felt so lost and inadequate, and this day he came to tell me the results. He said, "I'd really like to tell you that your husband will change one day and things will get better, but I can't. He may never change. I've tried to hear from the Lord for you, but I really don't know what to say to you, except to tell you to get close to the Lord."

That was really the last straw!! I was not just *in* this wretched situation, but there was no hope of *ever* getting out of it! This was how the entire rest of my life was going to look! I think people must have been able to see the smoke coming out of my ears. I thought for sure over the next few days that I would simply explode any second. I could not accept that my commitment to love someone for life, a relationship that was supposed to bring us mutual support and satisfaction, had turned into a sentence of life imprisonment in an armed camp with my worst enemy. For the first time in my life, I was even mad at God! How could He trap me like this. No divorce, indeed! He knew this was all going to happen. And to think I'd thought I had a vision of Jesus melding the two of us into one. Well, it certainly was going to take every bit of His great power to do that from here, wasn't it! Now, my decision wasn't what to do to put a marriage back together, but what I had to do even to survive. It was truly my darkest hour.

The pastor had said to get closer to God. That was not the most attractive option. I was right on the edge of blaming God for the whole mess. But God wouldn't quite let me get away with that. He kept reminding me of the ways He had already helped me. He kept showing me His promises of refuge and love. I slowly realized that I could not turn from Him. He was, in fact, my only hope. Meanwhile, I went through days of torture looking for some way to survive intact. Divorce, separation, and insanity all came under scrutiny. Surely God had an open door or window for me – somewhere.

Then a new thought occurred to me. If my husband wouldn't change, maybe I could change. At first that didn't sound too appealing. After all, I wasn't the one who needed to change, he was. I basically liked who I was. What should I do? Change for the worse, become more like my enemy? No! That was unacceptable. Maybe I could just change for the better, I mean stop worrying about whether my husband changed or not. Give up on him and start thinking only about who I was compared to who I really should be. It would mean giving up on our marriage ever becoming what I believed God said it should be. It would be a very painful decision. Change is always painful. But then, could anything be as painful as staying where I was? No, it couldn't.

So, I started a new life, focused on making me a better person. The decision made; I took the first few steps. I signed up for counseling. I joined a support group for dysfunctional families. I decided to have different responses to my husband when we argued. And I was amazed. I thought my stand was decidedly selfish, looking at only me, but I found that God somehow blessed the decision to change and gave me new responses when I needed them. My perspective on the problems switched dramatically, and, most important of all, I began to see many ways in which I really needed to change. In fact, it was not long before I came to the place where I saw

that my own problems were far worse than those of my husband.

Over the next two years, I discovered just how severely I had responded to the childhood trauma of losing my mother and being placed in a boarding school. I discovered I had created a whole other world of people in my mind that I did not consciously know was there. And I began to be healed of all the chaos that comes of not growing up at the right time. I began to be whole for the first time in 40 years. Also, I realized that my husband had stood by my side for twelve years, married to a crazy lady who was only six years old inside her head. I began to see him as faithful and steady and deserving of my love. It was a new start, indeed.

No, I did not take all the blame on myself. He wasn't perfect and had many changes to make, also. But since I accepted the severity of my part of the problem, the tension in the relationship relaxed to give us room to work out all of our problems.

It wasn't an instantaneous solution. The process of growing to emotional adulthood took time. And the marriage was still not perfect, but it was far from the mess it was before my decision to allow myself to be changed. We both began to actively work at improving our relationship and found new grounds for affection and respect for one another. We both made Jesus the center point and the standard for our lives. God used His great power to bring us into a healthier relationship.

Today, when I look back, I realize, had I not made that decision, as difficult as it was, my life might still be locked in that terrible prison camp. I also realize that my pastor had, indeed, heard from the Lord for me. He had heard and delivered exactly the words I needed to hear to allow God to change my life for the better. I praise God for His great love, that He showed the way to a new freedom I had never anticipated. It is much easier to make difficult decisions today because I have seen God's faithfulness in the most difficult decision I ever made.

> *"How can you say to your brother, 'Let me take the speck out of your eye,' when all the time there is a plank in your own eye."*
>
> Matthew 7:4

GOD OF LIFE

My God is the God of Life. How must my silence,
When He has told me to speak,
Tear at His tender heart.
I've leveled judgment of continued death,
On one to whom He would have proclaimed new life.

My God is the God of Life.
How must my determined shyness,
When He has told me to be bold,
Frustrate the all-powerful Lord,
As I allow continued destruction to reign,
Where He would have given restoration.

My God is the God of Life.
How must my angry bitterness,
When He has asked me to forgive,
Anger my loving Savior as I leave
My brother in Satan's bondage,
When He would have loosed him to Salvation.

LIFE!

My God is the God of Life
How He must cry over my choices for death.
For the death and destruction and bondage.
Of my arrogant disobedience,
Brings death to His Life within my spirit,
Just as it destroys the life He would send to others.

Lord, you are the God of Life.
Let your heart of mercy give me one more chance.
Work your life into me, that I may obey,
So no tinge of death would mar
My mirrored image of your glorious life.
And others might come to life through me.

ALONE NOW

There was a time when I was alone.
No matter how many people were around,
I was always alone.
My heart and soul cried out
To be a part of something, anything.
Yet, even in the midst of everything,
Inside myself I was alone.

> *"...the Lord your God goes with you; He will never leave you or forsake you."*
>
> Deuteronomy 31:6b

Then I met you, Jesus,
And my point of view
Began to change.

> *"I know the Lord is always with me. I will not be shaken, for He is right beside me."*
>
> Psalm 16:8 NLT

Though alone was still
The worst thing I could be,
I began to know I no longer had to be it.
For no matter how alone I was
I could always be with you.

Now alone has a new richness and beauty.
It is an opportunity to be with You.
It is a time of breathless intimacy with Joy,
It's fullness, completion, a desired privacy
With the Love of my life.

JOY!

NEW CHILD

For so many years I saw myself
As a frightened child,
Afraid, hiding, dirty,
Unloved, needy, inside.
Wanting so much to grow up,
But unable to go anywhere.
Trying so hard to be
What I thought I should be,
But unable to do anything.

But now the child I see inside is happy,
Skipping, smiling,
Laughing, even playful.
No longer afraid, but excited.
No longer dirty and unloved,
But clean—in her pinafore dress
And black patent shoes—
And loved and loving.
Eager to go and grow and do.
Free to be a child, Lord,
Because I am the child of You.

RESPONSE

I always used to be,
Or think of me, as a response,
Others did and I responded.
Now, I see that, in reality,
I am a stimulus, like it or not,
Even when I only respond,
For others respond to me.

> *"Do not conform to the pattern of this world but be transformed by the renewing of your mind."*
>
> Romans 12:2

As I let God change me,
I change others, too.
I change my stimulus, and that
Makes them change their response to me.
And then, I am able to change my response to them,
Then we are both free.
I am free to be responsible for me,
And I free them to be responsible for themselves.

Responsible means being able to respond
But it implies so very much more.
Being able to make decisions and choices.
Having resources.
Being free to do the right thing.

> *"We are God's handiwork, created in Christ Jesus to do good works, which God prepared for us in advance to do."*
>
> Ephesians 2:10

OLD DEPTHS

Once, I dwelt in the depths,
Breathing in the air of loneliness and despair,
Existing in the darkness of chaos and emptiness,
Until I let you, Jesus, come in and light up my life.

You lifted me out of that darkness, and now,
You have filled me up to brimming over,
So that all my depths are transformed from emptiness
Into storehouses filled with love
and joy and peace.

JOY!

NEW DEPTHS

From my beautiful new, Jesus built, dwelling place,
On the quiet mountain top of peace,
I experience a richness of depths I've never known
before,
The depths of the mystery and glory of Your Self.

The rich, inviting depths bring me more joy.
Than the depths of darkness gave me pain,
And I rejoice in anticipation of a lifetime and eternity
Spent exploring and plumbing the depths of Your love.

Thank you, Lord,
That You are who and what You are.
That your creating did not end with the world,
But continues within our hearts and spirits,
Whenever we release them to You

INVERSION

As a teen, I, too, thought myself
Wise and wonderful,
And found the rules were made
For everyone else but me.
At forty-nine, I realize
What a child I still am,
Especially compared to God.
Even today, it takes His wisdom,
And wonderfulness,
To make anything of me.

"If any of you lacks wisdom, you should ask God, who gives generously to all without finding fault, and it will be given to you."

James 1:5

POINT OF VIEW

> *"If we claim to be without sin, we deceive ourselves and the truth is not in us."*
>
> 1 John 1:8

I am a good person,
I don't lie or cheat or steal,
Don't smoke or drink. I'm good"
I almost convinced myself.

Then, that voice began to sting.
"You lie to yourself.
You cheat on My time.
You steal your companionship from Me."

"I'm so very sorry, Lord.
I never saw it as forgetting You.
Can You help me turn around and change?"

"Be glad to."
"Thanks."

> *"If we confess our sins, he is faithful and just and will forgive us our sins and purify us from all unrighteousness."*
>
> 1 John 1:9

PURPOSE FOR ME

> *"And we know that in all things God works for the good of those who love Him, who are called according to His purpose."*
>
> Romans 8:28

Why did I have to be crazy, Lord?
It wasn't fun. You know that, Lord.
Couldn't you have stopped or changed it, Lord?
Yes, but it wouldn't have been the same.
You mean, like the man that Jesus healed,
Who had been born blind?
It was for the greater glory of God?

What was that, Lord?
It doesn't stop there?
You can see farther than I can?
What does that mean?
Does God gain glory from healing me
If no one ever hears of it?
It's not for the healing itself
That the sickness existed,
But for the glory that will come to
You, As others hear about it,
Others, who know the same pain,
Who can use my words to find Your healing.
Hallelujah, Lord!!!

Lord, if even one other person,
Hurting and sick,
Can find freedom from pain,
And find peace and joy,
And the love and acceptance I've found in You,
Because of my pain,
Then it's <u>more</u> than all right with me.
It's cause for rejoicing and singing and shouting,
For dancing and praising your name, forever.

> *"His disciples asked Him, 'Rabbi, who sinned, this man or his parents…?'*
>
> *'Neither this man nor his parents sinned,' said Jesus, 'but this happened so that the works of God might be displayed in Him.'"*
>
> John 9:2-3

WIND MEMORIES

Walking the chill, windy California shore,
Wrapped in sweats and jacket, hood and gloves,
Sore knees pushing against the "moon walk" rocks,
Cold wind driving into me with each step!

"Bob, that's all the wind I can take.
I'll see you back at the van.
At last! I can slow down,
And face *away* from the wind!
It was the wind that got me.
I've always had trouble with the wind in my face.

Memory flash of my sickly little self,
Thin as a bean,
So weak that the wind picked me up,
And carried me a ways.

When I need to do something,
And the wind pushes me back, I have to fight it.
It's as though it could defeat me.
That's it!! I'm afraid!
I'm afraid the wind will beat me.

Don't be afraid, the warm gentle,
Loving, familiar voice says:
Says, implores, informs, assures, that's all.
But, suddenly, that wall of cold wind,
That seemed to be such an obstacle to me,
Felt warm, like a warm, strong hand,
Caressing my face, affectionately,
A hand I can trust and lean on.

Next time I have the wind in my face, Lord,
I'll have this beautiful memory to shape my response.
Fear has been wiped out,
And its place has been filled by love.
Confidence and peace reside
Where once a panic reigned.
Wind may become my favorite thing.
Thank you, Lord.

An important note:

The following year, we moved to Newfoundland, Canada, to a place where the wind was often nearly 50 mph.
30 mph was thought of as a breeze. And, in a storm, the wind would turn over narrow gauge railroad cars and tractor trailers.

I loved it!

GOD HUG

Cats are absolutely extravagant in seeking and giving attention. My cat, Joy, leaps onto my lap at the slightest provocation, placing herself into whatever position will most interfere with my work of the moment. Ignoring her just doesn't work. She rubs her face against my hand, puts her tail in my face, kneads my leg with her claws, chews on my pen. And if I remove her to the floor, she's back in three seconds. She simply demands I give her love. I grab hold of her and scratch her chin and ears, rub her tummy and repeatedly tell her how beautiful and wonderful she is. She responds by twisting and turning so I have access to all the soft sensitive areas. And, of course, she purrs, a loud, deep, steady purr that says I've made her just as happy as she could possibly be. My frustration and irritation fade into satisfaction and peace. I have received more than I have given.

But my mind dwells on the incident. There have been a few times when I have so wanted attention that I actively demanded it. I went to God and called Him Daddy; told Him all the ways I needed His attention. I hoped He could **somehow** send me someone to hold me and give me all the attention I wanted. I was afraid He would be irritated, think me a baby, and dismiss me.

Instead of rejecting me, or sending a person, God, himself, gave me a hug! I don't really know how to say it, but He made me feel as though He and I were the only two people in the universe at that moment, that He was holding on to me and He would never let me go. Without words, He let me know that I belonged to Him, and I was precious to Him. By then I was tearing up from joy because of His sweetness and love. Then He let me know that the very fact that I desired His attention and would come to Him for my needs was very pleasing to Him. I received so much more than I expected.

When this world gets to be too much for you, when you feel you can't or don't want to keep going, I recommend going to your heavenly Father and telling Him how you feel. He won't reject you and He just might give you a God Hug, just because you thought of Him.

"May Your loving devotion comfort me, I pray, according to your promise to your servant. May Your compassion come to me, that I may live, for Your law is my delight."

Psalm 119:76-77, Berean Study Bible

PROGRESS

> *"Search me, God, and know my heart; test me and know my anxious thoughts. See if there is any offensive way in me, and lead me in the way everlasting."*
>
> Psalm 139:23-24

I see the need for change in her,
And want to help, to grow her up into that place.
I know it's right and Godly, so I begin
To tell her, and entreat her, pray for her,
And tell her yet again.
But she doesn't budge,
And I lose my temper, then pray some more,
And start again,
With just as much success as before.
'Till I'm at my wits' end.

Then, one day, thinking about some other thing,
That's been milling about inside my brain,
I make a connection about changes *I* need to make.
Suddenly, before I can even put that thought to work,
The change in *her* is made.

There is no room for "I told you so",
Or even "What took you so long?"
Just a sigh of relief and "Thank you, Lord,"
And "That's wonderful!" For it takes your breath away.

But what caused that change to happen,
And why did it show up just now?
No! It couldn't be!
You mean, while I was trying for growth in her,
You were holding on 'til you could see
Growth in me?
Help me see, Lord. Help me see.

"Then neither do I condemn you.
Go and sin no more."

John 8:11, NKJV

TO BE

Lord, please help me to be.
Be content in Your presence,
Be worry-free,
Be caught up in Your wonder,
Not thinking of me.

Be lost in Your joy,
Be focused true,
Be blind to distraction,
Centered on You.

With hands that are busy
With what must be done,
But a mind and a heart
That can see only One.

Our spirits are joined,
And the joy is so great,
Lord, I want not to visit,
But TO BE in this state.

> *"But seek first His kingdom and His righteousness and all these will be given to you as well."*
>
> Matthew 6:33

LANGUAGE ENCOUNTER

A psalm, a song, a word or a verse, brought to life today
To open our eyes to Your workings,
Now rattles around in our hearts and heads,
Long after the reason for its coming is clear.

It rattles and nags for months or years,
'Til we think for sure it will never be gone.
Then, of a sudden, we open our eyes
To see in the phrase a big surprise.
That very same verse You brought to pass—back then,
You fulfilled it again, just now.

But this time it's on a different scale,
The meaning is different, the point is all new.
But the word still applies, not a syllable changed.
You've only expanded our minds, it seems.
To look at the thing from another perspective
And see a whole new view.
How marvelous of you!

Now here's where the beauty gets even better.
That same little word still sits in our heads.
It hasn't gone, but this time we're wise.
We can see what's coming.
We can watch You work
As You turn that word 'round again.
And make it new and true once more

Hey! I'm learning from this.
It's not just that single word or phrase
I'm starting to think of in brand new ways.
I'm looking at life and all that's a part of it
In ways I'd never thought of before.
And just by seeing multiple meanings
In a phrase You gave me long ago,
I'm starting to think, to live and to do,
In ways that are bigger and fuller and better.

> *"Let the wise listen and add to their learning and let the discerning get guidance."*
>
> Proverbs 1:5

It's beautiful, Lord! I love it.
The way ideas expand and grow
When You get hold of them,
Says so much about who You are,
And what happens to us,
When we let You get hold of us

ADVENTURE

> *"But those who hope in the Lord will renew their strength. They will soar on wings like eagles; they will run and not grow weary, they will walk and not be faint."*
>
> Isaiah 40:31

My years with You have been
Such a marvelous journey,
And it is _so_ good being
Where I am today.
Not because I've come
To such a marvelous place,
(Which I have – the me I see
Has changed so much,
And anyplace with You, Lord
Is indescribably delicious)
But because I'm not afraid
To travel farther.

Like Bilbo Baggins,
The thought of change and adventure
Has gotten into my blood.
I'm looking
forward
To all the years yet to come
That will be filled with spiritual adventure with you.

THE OTHER SIDE

Hey, Mom,
Why can't I go see that new movie?
Everybody else is going!

Honey, there's so much
Anger and violence in it,
I wouldn't want it to hurt your spirit.

Then why do you and Daddy fight?
And why do you yell at me?
Those things hurt my spirit, too.
Uh. . .I. . .I'm so sorry, my sweet.

Sometimes, we all get so caught up
In our own anger and hurt,
We can't see we hurt others, too.
I'll ask God to help me change.
Will you forgive us? Please?

"My sacrifice, O God, is a broken spirit. A broken and contrite heart you, God, will not despise."

Psalm 51:17

DIVORCE

I was raised believing that God hates divorce, and we should avoid it at all costs. Moses only allowed divorce because people were killing their spouses so they could remarry, or as the Bible says because of our cruelty to one another. And when I was married, I would get frustrated and angry and that little temptation to think divorce could be an answer would be there. God would always stop me and remind me about no divorce. Until one day He didn't. I still fought to apply a Biblical bandage to the problem, but my husband did not want to abide by biblical principles, so at 68 years old, I had to end our 40 years of marriage through divorce.

My husband and I got married to solve a problem and we stayed married because we made a commitment and that's what you do when you make a commitment. Don't get me wrong, we were in love, but we let the urgency of our problems dictate our behavior. Neither of us had come to know the Lord at that time, and we were trying to solve problems that were so much bigger than we knew, in our own strength. That just doesn't work for very long. You see, we were both reasonably intelligent on an academic scale, but neither one of us had a very high emotional IQ. We were not only from emotionally dry and broken backgrounds, but we both also tended to be more than a little naïve about how to live life. We didn't really consider that our backgrounds were going to affect our futures.

Things went from pretty good to terrible, until we finally met Jesus and started trying to walk as Christians. Jesus healed me of some emotional problems, which improved the relationship for a while, but there were still issues and I was slow to admit that I had to be the one to change to improve the situation. That's when I discovered I was suffering from what used to be called Multiple Personality Syndrome and began 18 months of psychological care and spiritual deliverance. As I grew emotionally, several aspects of our relationship improved for a while.

However, as one might expect from our emotionally dry and broken backgrounds, our physical relationship had its problems, lacking the expected or desirable emotional intimacy. Moreover, I had pain which eventually became severe. We didn't talk about it much and, unfortunately, the medical profession was neither sympathetic nor very helpful. Eventually I could no longer handle the pain that substituted for what should have been the joyous part of marriage and that aspect became only an occasional event rather than a relationship. This left me feeling totally worthless as a woman. My husband's response was to find relief on the internet and that exploded into Nigerian romance scams that stole all our retirement and created a sizeable debt. The marriage ended as much as anything else, to protect me from further disaster, when he refused every effort toward counselling, refused to get a job to attempt to pay off the debt, and declared he did not want to do things the biblical way.

I pray for him regularly and we talk when appropriate. My desire is to see him come back to a godly relationship with Jesus.

MY EVERYTHING GOD

If my God were any less loving

than I know Him to be,

If He were any less kind,

Any less merciful,

Any less patient,

Any less knowing,

Any less powerful,

Any less creative

Than I know Him to be,

I would be either long ago dead,

or on a trash heap somewhere.

How can I ever thank Him enough

for being everything He says He is!

EVERYTHING!

WHERE AM I NOW?

My life has had its ups and downs. And that has held true even after all of God's miracles. But whatever the circumstances, God has been with me every day, even when the day is one I would not choose to remember.

When I had to divorce after 40 years, at 68 years old, and came away with nothing but a part-time job, things looked a bit bleak. But, my faithful, on-time God provided, and I slowly regained some stability. And while I knew my past security was gone, and could never be completely recovered, for a while it looked like I would be able to live some kind of average life, with shelter, food, transportation and paying my bills without too much trouble. Then the world turned upside down!

A housing shortage in Salt Lake City brought the price of even the smallest apartment up above my ability to pay. I moved to a less expensive area, but as I watched the process continue, I realized that there was no safe place. Sometime in my elder years, I was going to be homeless, living out of my car. I was terrified! I knew God could do all things, but my human mind could not grasp how He could solve this problem.

Well, thanks to the only mutual friend I and my ex have, we ended up on the Dr. Phil Show, (Dr. Phil: Robert and Jeremi) where Dr. Phil closed out the last segment by saying, "If someone wants to start a GoFundMe for this lady to get a house, I won't say nay". I didn't believe it. I did not think God worked that way. Surely, He wasn't going to give me a house through Dr. Phil. But, just on the outside chance that it could raise a few thousand dollars, I wrote up my story and waited.

Once the program aired, I did not have long to wait. Over the next few weeks, more than 2300 people donated to my cause, and I recognized God can do that if He wants. It wasn't long until I realized I could indeed own a house and be freed from the greedy apartment rental business. Yea God! And many prayers and thanks were offered for my donors.

As soon as Covid19 travel restrictions were sufficiently lifted, I found a modest home in a small mid-western town. (And for those who know my story, no, my ex did not get any of the donated funds.) I settled in and found a church that knows what it means to love and befriend others. I got involved in the church and began to feel God had not only given me a house but had brought me to a home. I was so blessed.

I continued to work full-time for a while but then had to go part-time. Then I faced a knee replacement operation and, once I was out of work for a while, it became very hard to find new employment, at 77, though I am still in good health and strong for my age. So, today I live happily in my God given home. My Social Security, like most people's, is not enough to meet my needs, and my small emergency fund is just that – small. So, I piece together whatever I can, to get by. And God continues to provide in ways I don't always understand.

While a part of me would rather have a more set and regular source of income, I am glad that I can daily watch God work His wonders in providing for all my needs. It's a little scary, but also exciting. This situation keeps me dependent on God and rejoicing in His continuing provision.

Without the trappings of worldly success, I still consider myself more fortunate than many. I know my gifting as a prayer warrior and I know my ultimate destination is eternity with the Lord God, Creator of the Universe and Jesus Christ, savior of all who will come to Him.

BECOMING NOTHING

"I am nothing."
How such a thought used to scare me silly,
Probably 'cause I felt it was true.
I didn't feel I really existed.
Didn't know who I was meant to be.
I was scared of nothing 'cause nothing was <u>me</u>.

Then I met You Jesus,
And all of those things just started to change.
I knew I was real. I knew I was special –
Handmade by You for a purpose You knew.

You're taking charge and healing and changing me.
Making me into what You know I can be.
And I stand by in awe-struck wonder,
As you weave the tapestry that is to be me.

Now I see that as I grow, Lord,
Becoming more whole,
Discovering your goals,
"Me" is no longer so important,
The power of the "I" is fading away.

I'm not thinking of the something
You're making of me.
Instead, I'm thinking
Of the wonders of my God.
I live, it says, and yet, not I,
But Christ that lives within me.
My **old man** died, and I died too.

> *"Anyone who loves their life will lose it, while anyone who hates their life in this world will keep it for eternal life."*
>
> John 12:25

Died to let my Jesus live in me.
The very thing I feared to become
Is what you're making me by your hand.

Now I am nothing but an empty vessel,
Desiring nothing but to be filled with Thee.
Now being nothing fills me with Joy.
For this kind of nothing surely is
The perfect nothing for me to be.

REASONS

There was a time when I did not want to go on. At 70 years old, I had just gotten divorced, after 40 years of marriage, and had walked away with nothing. I was working a full-time job in retail for very little money. I was wearing two knee braces and using a cane. And my only daughter decided to block my calls and refuse to talk to me. (I am a born-again Christian, and she decided she wanted to align herself with the morals of today.) Here I was, working myself to death to get back on my feet, and those who had been the nearest and dearest to me had somehow turned into strangers. What was the point?! I would have been delighted to leave this life and go to be with the Lord, the only one who knew and loved me and would never let me go.

But the Lord would not hear of it. He reminded me that I love to see His sunsets and sunrises. I see His hand in the beauty of nature, and I take joy in seeing Him transform lives around me.

Those were the reasons I should continue living. It may not seem like much to some. There are no warm bodies to give you hugs, no children or grandchildren to carry your name and values down the ages. But, when the God of the universe says that He wants you to stay alive because you like His handiwork, how do you argue with Him? So, I said OK. I will stay here and take joy in who you are, until you are ready for me to come to you. If it is your will, it is good enough for me.

Now when things begin to seem too much, I just remember that God says He wants me to be alive to see His beauty, and I go look at some of His beautiful artwork. And I think "It is enough!" It is enough to keep me happy here yet always longing to be there.

BIRTHDAY GIFT

Another year has passed, and I still marvel
How you have taken the needy, dirty, unloved child
I was at thirty-five and turned her into
A functional adult who can give and receive love.

And the difference is You, Lord.
You came into my life and loved me,
Changed me, healed me, cleansed me, and set me free.
So many years ago you showed me the child I was,
And the child of You that you would make of me.

Today I see, again, Your word is true.
You have made me over into that second child,
Who joyfully takes Your hand,
And walks the path of life with You.

> *"I will give you a new heart and put a new spirit in you; I will remove from you your heart of stone and give you a heart of flesh."*
>
> Ezekiel 36:26

How can there be enough praise in the universe
To give you all the thanks You are due

For the wonders of the works You've done
In changing one small, unworthy creature
Into someone who can smile at You.
Thank you, Lord.

If you give birthday gifts, dear Lord
There's one I would ask of You.
Please reach out to all those other
Frightened, hiding, dirty, unloved, needy little children,

Whatever their ages may be,
And do for them the marvelous thing
You've done for me.
Thank You Lord!

Thank You Lord!!!

DREAMABLE

Unfulfilled dream? Impossible?
It is both, yet neither.
For I dream of the constant presence of God.

I have a bit of it, here and there,
But that's just not enough.
I hunger and thirst for so much more.

I want to be surrounded by His glory,
Seeing only Him,
And desiring to see nothing else.

I want to breathe His very breath,
Drinking Him in, absorbing Him,
Having His nature seep from my pores.

I want to be heart-to-heart with Him,
My very essence pulsing
In time with His desires.

I, who once could not bear
To come into God's presence,
Dare to desire to be lost
In that very place,
Now and forever, Amen!

> *"You make known to me the path of life; you will fill me with joy in your presence, with eternal pleasures at your right hand."*.
>
> Psalm 16:11

DREAMS

I thought I knew about dreams.
To me, they have always been clouds,
Fluffy, fleeting, high above me,
Floating in the sunlight.
Cool, distant, intangible.
I did not realize I had not yet begun
To understand the nature of a dream.

Today, a dream enfolds my heart.
It is close, warm, solid, alive and organic.
It surrounds me,
Holding, supporting, protecting me.

It urges me on, gently leading me
Ever onward toward my goal--
A goal of existing, being constantly,
Always in the presence of God.

CHOOSING LIFE

"Choose Life!" It's one of those slogans that no one can oppose. It is simple, clear, positive, with all the attributes one could desire for a quick easy expression to summarize the answer to a host of problems. But don't be fooled by its glib sound. While choosing life is indeed positive, and an answer to a host of problems, it is not always simple, or clear and, in most cases, it is neither quick, nor easy.

When the addict turns from his dependency to choose life, he chooses, moment by moment, to resist that constant temptation to hide from life in some kind of drugged state, knowing the struggle will always be with him. He faces years, decades, of a daily battle in which he continually makes himself vulnerable to all the hurts of this world, though they have already brought him down to the point of addiction. He will need to be constantly alert to the activity around him, which can push him into making that other choice, the choice of death in the oblivion of drug-induced non-existence. Ten-step programs stress that one-day-at-a-time aspect of recovery, because while the addict must consciously commit to the continual long-term battle, dwelling on its unrelenting, forever nature virtually insures defeat. And for the most part, the addict will have to fight his battle alone. Others simply will not perceive the struggle that goes on within him. Only God will be able, really, to hold his hand and comfort the depth of his hurt. No, it is neither quick nor easy.

The single pregnant woman who chooses life makes a commitment to nurture another life for years. It may mean that her own dreams will be put on hold for two decades or more. She will have to change her perception of who she is. She'll no longer be Betty, or an up-and-coming lawyer or designer. She'll be Mommy, 24 hours every day. And while the baby will come though she takes no action, the choice of life will not come through non-choices or happenstance. It will require her active consent, not blaming others, but accepting responsibility. For her, choosing life may mean that she'll struggle just to feed her child, having to make hard choices between giving nurture or sustenance. And she, too, will be alone in her struggle, with only God to really know how hard it is. Facing the choice between this and a life of minimal responsibility or, perhaps, maximum financial return in a good profession, the single girl raised in poverty and aching to find another way of life, surely could see the choice of a quick trip to the doctor's office as the choice for life. No, it's not simple and it isn't always as clear as we'd like to think.

Choosing life is an active, up front, in your face, demanding kind of process that requires facing pain and hardships of our own volition. It is the hardest choice we have to make. But it is also the best choice we have the opportunity to make. It is the choice that leads to learning and growing and self-discipline. It is the choice that leads to overcoming our worst fears and greatest obstacles. It is the choice that leads us out of the darkness of our many hiding places into the light of mature choices and healthy living. Most of all it is the choice that helps us be transformed into the image of God's own son, Jesus Christ, who is the Way, the Truth, and the Life.

However, there is one way of choosing life that is very different. Yes, it requires total commitment. But it offers total victory. It is choosing the life offered by Jesus Christ. For choosing Jesus is choosing to allow the Lord to help you in every aspect of your life. He always supplies the power to accomplish whatever goal He asks you to seek. And He desires to heal the underlying problems of your life, so that you can become whole and complete in Him.

I chose life in Jesus many years ago, and it has been worth the commitment I made in doing so. It hasn't meant that I no longer had any troubles, but He has been an ever-present help in every trouble I have faced. Even when I have fallen back into old habits of trying to escape the reality of life, He has been faithful to forgive and encourage me, and to put my feet back on the right path. I encourage you to choose the life found in Jesus Christ, as you face the need to deal with whatever other choices for life you need to make. Those other choices will come so much easier with the help of the Lord of the universe at your side.

YOU TOUCHED MY LIFE

> *"And we know that in all things God works for the good of those who love Him, who are called according to His purpose."*
>
> Romans 8:28

You touched my life,
And I may have thought
it was good or bad,
You touched my life,
And it may have made me
happy or sad.
But, whatever it was,
it became
A part of who I am,
And I have reason to
be grateful to you;

For God has taken all those touches,
Good or bad, or happy or sad,
And has worked them out
For His kingdom's glory.
He has made from them the spice for my life,
Which makes me able to write these words.

He used them all to make me
A child who can praise His name,
To give me a heart that hungers after Him,
To make me one who desires most
To see others healed,
Of the hurt and pain of the kind I've seen.

AN OPPORTUNITY

> *"If we confess our sins, He is faithful and just and will forgive us our sins and purify us from all unrighteousness."*
>
> 1 John 1:9

If, as you read these works you recognized a need for change in your life, I urge you to turn to Jesus and say this prayer:

Jesus, I want you to come into my heart and change my life. I admit that I need a savior, and I repent of anything in my life that does not agree with your will for me. Please lead me to a place where I can receive support, and experience the reality of being a member of the family of Jesus Christ.

> *"For God so loved the world that He gave His one and only Son, that whoever believes in Him shall not perish but have eternal life. For God did not send His Son into the world to condemn the world, but to save the world through Him.*
>
> John 3:16-17

ABOUT THE AUTHOR

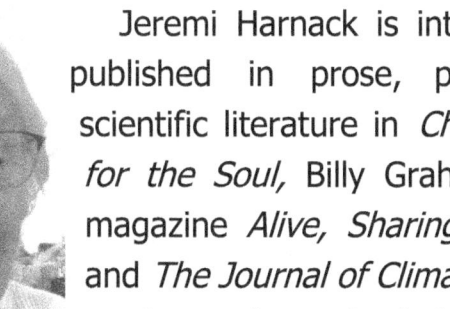 Jeremi Harnack is internationally published in prose, poetry, and scientific literature in *Chicken Soup for the Soul,* Billy Graham's youth magazine *Alive, Sharing Magazine,* and *The Journal of Climatology.*

Jeremi has a Bachelor of Arts in English Education and a Master of Science in Meteorology. When her daughter was born, she put her scholastic career on hold and homeschooled her all the way to college, where she received advanced placement.

In her 40-plus years as a Christian, she has been a facilitator of women's groups, led prayer meetings, taught children's church, and was the head of a prayer ministry of a medium-sized church for ten years.

She loves to travel, having visited most of the states and provinces of North America. She loves walking and dancing in worship to the Lord.

Jeremi currently attends The Hill Church in Stockton, Missouri.

www.ingramcontent.com/pod-product-compliance
Lightning Source LLC
Chambersburg PA
CBHW051351040426
42453CB00023B/273